THE ULTIMATE

"YO MAMA"

JOKE BOOK

THE ULTIMATE

"YO MAMA"

JOKE BOOK

Collected by
Guy A. De Marco

Villainous Press
Denver, Colorado

THE ULTIMATE "YO MAMA" JOKE BOOK

Copyright © 2013 Villainous Press

ISBN: 978-1-62225-031-8

Book Design by RuneWright, LLC
www.RuneWright.com

Published by
Villainous Press, an imprint of
The Publishing Consortium, LLC
PO Box 473190
Aurora CO 80047

Villainous Press Trade Paperback Edition December 2013
Printed in the USA
www.VillainousPress.com

Contents

YO MAMA'S SO SKINNY...

If your mama can play hide and seek by hiding behind a fencepost, this chapter is for you.

Sayeth not anything against my mama, for mine fury shalt be glorious as I pummelest thou about the head and shoulders.

King Edward the VIII

Yo mama's so skinny that she turned sideways and disappeared.

Yo mama's so skinny that she hula hoops with a Cheerio.

Yo mama's so skinny that she has to wear a belt with spandex.

Yo mama's so skinny that she swallowed a meatball and thought she was pregnant.

Yo mama's so skinny that she can see out of a peephole with both eyes at the same time.

Yo mama's so skinny that she uses a Band-Aid as a maxi-pad.

Yo mama's so skinny, you cut your lip when she breast-fed you.

Yo mama's so skinny that you can save her from drowning by tossing her a Fruit Loop.

Yo mama's so skinny that she has to run around in the shower to get wet.

Yo mama's so skinny, her full-time job is being a wind sock.

Yo mama's so skinny that when she wore her yellow dress, she looked like a #2 pencil.

Yo mama's so skinny that if she had a sesame seed on her head, she'd look like a push pin.

Yo mama's so skinny, she went to the library and someone thought she was a bookmark.

Yo mama's so skinny that her nipples touch.

Yo mama's so skinny that I could blind-fold her with dental floss.

Yo mama's so skinny that she looks like a microphone stand.

Yo mama's so skinny that she only has one stripe on her pajamas.

Yo mama's so skinny that she can dodge rain drops.

Yo mama's so skinny that she inspires crack whores to diet.

Yo mama's so skinny that she uses Chapstick for deodorant.

Yo mama's so skinny, her skeleton is transparent.

Yo mama's so skinny that she goes paragliding with a Dorito.

Yo mama's so skinny, when the wind blows, she sounds like a flute.

Yo mama's so skinny that if she turned sideways and stuck out her tongue, she would look like a zipper.

Yo mama's so skinny, she was the influence for discovering graphene.

Yo mama's so skinny that she goes hot tubbing with the Mini Wheats Man.

Yo mama's so skinny that when she takes a bath and lets the water out, her toes get caught in the drain.

Yo mama's so skinny, when she went out in a wind storm, she ended up in Australia.

Yo mama's so skinny that her bra fits better when she wears it backwards.

Yo mama's so skinny that she had to stand in the same place twice to cast a shadow.

Yo mama's so skinny that if she had a yeast infection she'd be a Quarter Pounder with Cheese.

Yo mama's so skinny that her pants only have one belt loop.

Yo mama's so skinny that if she had dreads I'd grab her by the ankles and use her to mop the floor.

Yo mama's so skinny that instead of calling her your parent, you call her transparent.

Yo mama's so skinny, when you sneeze, she ends up in the next county.

Yo mama's so skinny, when she was tackled by a linebacker in gym class, she sliced him in half.

Yo Mama's So Dirty...

...and we don't mean dirty-minded.

Four score and seven years go, the south insulted my mama. Now look what happened...

Abraham Lincoln

Yo mama's so dirty, she calls the cat box the clean room.

Yo mama's so dirty, she can't pass emissions.

Yo mama's so dirty, when she dipped her toes in the Mississippi river, she created a dam from the mud.

Yo mama's house is so dirty that when it caught on fire, it burned for 47 years.

Yo mama's so dirty, they found two raccoons living underneath her toenails.

Yo mama's so dirty, she was banned from the sewage plant because of sanitation concerns.

Yo mama's so dirty, she lost 20lbs after taking a shower.

Yo mama's so dirty, you can't tell where the dirt ends and where she begins.

Yo mama's house is so dirty, you hang out in the fireplace to keep from getting too dirty.

Yo mama's so dirty that she has to creep up on bathwater.

Yo mama's hair is so dirty, she raised five sets of birds and never found the nest on her head.

Yo mama's so dirty that even Swamp Thing told her to take a shower.

Yo mama's so dirty that the US Government uses her bath water as a chemical weapon.

Yo mama's so dirty that when she tried to take a bath, the water jumped out and said "I'll wait."

Yo mama's house is so dirty, she has to wipe her feet before she goes outside.

Yo mama's house is so dirty, she has to get daily tetanus shots.

Yo mama's so dirty, she makes mud look clean.

Yo mama's house is so dirty, they found Jimmy Hoffa's body in the basement.

Yo mama's house was so dirty, when it caught fire you could see it from space.

Yo mama's house is so dirty, she has more sand than the Sahara in the carpet.

Yo mama's house is so dirty, rats avoid it.

Yo mama's house is so dirty, the roaches held a protest rally outside.

Yo Mama's So Hairy...

Is their mother related to Cousin It from the Addams Family? This is the chapter for you.

Oh, yeah, yo mama's a hottie.

Chewbacca

Yo mama's so hairy, she looks like she has Bigfoot in a headlock.

Yo mama's so hairy, Bigfoot makes passes at her.

Yo mama's so hairy, she shaves her legs with a lawn mower.

Yo mama's so hairy, she dated Chewbacca.

Yo mama's so hairy, she was Chewbacca's stunt double, and didn't need a costume.

Yo mama's so hairy, she has braids on her back.

Yo mama's so hairy, she gets marriage proposals from dwarves.

Yo mama's so hairy, she won a "biggest mustache" contest.

Yo mama's so hairy, she gets a five o'clock shadow at 10AM.

Yo mama's so hairy, she uses her toe hair as shoelaces.

Yo mama's so hairy, she hides her purse in her armpits.

Yo mama's so hairy, the bearded lady at the carnival says, "Damn!"

Yo mama's so hairy, people think her hairy chest is her beard.

Yo mama's so hairy, she makes Grimace from McDonalds look good.

Yo mama has so much hair on her upper lip that she braids it.

Yo mama's so hairy that Bigfoot wants to take HER picture!

Yo mama's so hairy that she looks like she has Buckwheat in a headlock.

Yo mama's so hairy that you almost died of rugburn at birth!

Yo mama's so hairy that they filmed "Gorillas in the Mist" in her shower!

Yo mama's so hairy that if she could fly she'd look like a magic carpet.

Yo mama's so hairy that she looks like Bigfoot in a tank top.

Yo mama's so hairy that she has afros on her nipples.

Yo mama's so hairy that when I took her to a pet store they locked her in a cage.

Yo mama's so hairy that she looks like a Chia pet with a sweater on.

Yo mama's so hairy that Jane Goodall follows her around.

Yo mama's so hairy that the only language she can speak is wookie.

Yo mama's so hairy that she shaves her legs with a weedwacker.

Yo mama's so hairy that if you shaved her legs, you could supply wigs for the entire Hair Club for Men.

Yo mama's so hairy that her armpits look like she has Don King in a headlock.

Yo mama's so hairy that she's got sideburns on her boobs.

Yo mama's so hairy Naruto thought she was a Summon.

Yo mama's so hairy and ugly that she got used as Ashitare's stunt double.

Yo mama's so hairy that she has to go to Furfest to meet a man.

Yo mama's nosehairs are so long that they make Bobobo jealous!

Yo mama's so hairy that she got a trim and lost 20 pounds.

Yo mama's so hairy that people run up to her and say "Chewbacca, can I get your autograph?"

Yo mama's so hairy that she gets mistaken for Chewbacca's cousin.

Yo mama's so hairy that two birds made nests in her armpits and she doesn't even know about it!

Yo mama's so hairy that when she's at a nude beach people think she's wearing a fur coat!

YO MAMA'S SO OLD...

Does she creak when she walks?

Yeah, it was a tough choice between yo mama and Eve.

Adam

Yo mama's so old, when she was told to act her age, she died.

Yo mama's so old that when she was in school, they didn't have history classes yet.

Yo mama's so old, her high school yearbook has a picture of Moses in it.

Yo mama's so old, her high school diploma was chiseled out of granite.

Yo mama's so old, she knew Fred Flintstone personally.

Yo mama's so old, she rode a dinosaur to school.

Yo mama's so old, her birth certificate says "expired."

Yo mama's so old, one of her pets came from Noah's Ark.

Yo mama's so old that she goes on carbon dates.

Yo mama's so old, her birth certificate is in Roman numerals.

Yo mama's so old, she knew the Burger King when he was a prince.

Yo mama's so old, she was best friends with Eve.

Yo mama's so old, she dated Adam.

Yo mama's so old, she played piano for silent movie theatres.

Yo mama's so old, her memory is in black and white.

Yo mama's so old, Jurrasic Park brought back memories.

Yo mama's so old, she called the cops when David and Goliath started to fight.

Yo mama's so old, she has hieroglyphics on her driving license.

Yo mama's so old, she has a first printing of the Ten Commandments.

Yo mama's so old, she has an autographed bible.

Yo mama's so old, her underwear is made out of brontosaurus skin.

Yo mama's so old, the only tablets she knows how to work had the Ten Commandments carved on them.

Yo mama's so old, she recalls when the Grand Canyon was just a small ditch.

Yo mama's so old, she remembers what life was like during the ice age.

Yo mama's so old, she went to an antique store and they kept her.

Yo mama's so old, she went to an antique auction and three people bid on her.

Yo mama's so old, she accidentally had a keg stuck in a glacier, and finally dug it out.

Yo mama's so old, she DJ'd at the Boston Tea Party.

Yo mama's so old, candles cost more than the cake.

Yo mama's so old, she farts dust.

Yo mama's so old, she has a job as a display in a museum.

Yo mama's so old, she wakes up with cobwebs in her eyes.

Yo mama's so old, she outlived Dracula.

Yo mama's so old, she saw Moses' baby bassinet floating by.

Yo mama's so old, she still has the wooden stands from the original Ten Commandment tablets.

Yo mama's so old, she went to claim her pottery from an archeological dig in Egypt.

Yo mama's so old, the last time she had a birthday cake she started the Chicago Fire.

Yo mama's so old, she reminisces when reading the Bible.

Yo mama's so old that her social security number is 1.

Yo mama's so old that she has Adam & Eve's autographs.

Yo mama's so old that she co-wrote the Ten Commandments.

Yo mama's so old she remembers when the Mayans published their calendar.

Yo mama's so old that she owes Fred Flintstone a food stamp.

Yo mama's so old that she drove a chariot to high school.

Yo mama's so old that she took her driver's test on a dinosaur.

Yo mama's so old that she baby-sat for Jesus.

Yo mama's so old that she knew Mr. Clean when he had an afro.

Yo mama's so old that she knew the Beetles when they were the New Kids on the Block.

Yo mama's so old that when God said "Let there be light" she was there to flick the switch.

Yo mama's so old that she needed a walker when Jesus was still in diapers.

Yo mama's so old that when Moses split the red sea, she was on the other side fishing.

Yo mama's so old that she learned to write on cave walls.

Yo mama's so old that she's mentioned in the shout out at the end of the bible.

Yo mama's so old that she planted the first tree at Central Park.

Yo mama's so old that she sat next to Jesus in third grade.

Yo mama's so old that she knew Cap'n Crunch while he was still a private.

Yo mama's so old that when she was born, the Dead Sea was just getting sick.

Yo mama's so old, when she breast feeds, people mistake her for a fog machine.

Yo mama's so old that when she was young rainbows were black and white.

Yo mama's so old that she was a waitress at the Last Supper.

Yo mama's so old that she owes Jesus a dollar.

Yo mama's so old that she ran track with dinosaurs.

Yo mama's so old, she used to babysit Dumbledore.

Yo mama's so old, her boobs look like two upside down Sorting Hats!

Yo mama's so old she gave Nicholas Flamel his first kiss.

Yo mama's so old she makes Dumbledore look like a teenager.

Yo mama's so old even Guinan refers to her as "old bag".

Yo mama's so old and fat they use her wrinkles as set terrain for Dragon Ball Z.

YO MAMA'S SO NASTY...

That's Nasty with a capital "N".

Yo mama's my idol!

Pigpen, a friend of Charlie Brown

Yo mama's so nasty, when I called her on my cell phone I got an ear infection.

Yo mama's so nasty, she started a foot fungus garden in her beard.

Yo mama's so nasty, she won the grandmaster award at Skanks of America.

Yo mama's so nasty, she leaves a puddle of fungus wherever she sits.

Yo mama's so nasty, she uses her ear mushrooms as earrings.

Yo mama's so nasty that she makes speed stick slow down.

Yo mama's so nasty that she brings crabs to the beach.

Yo mama's so nasty that that pours salt water down her pants to keep her crabs fresh.

Yo mama's so nasty that the fishery pays her to stay away.

Yo mama's so nasty that she only changes her drawers once every 10000 miles.

Yo mama's so nasty that a skunk smelled her and passed out.

Yo mama's so nasty that I chatted with her on Facebook and she gave me a real-life virus.

Yo mama's so nasty that her boobs leak sour milk.

Yo mama's so nasty that she has to use Right Guard and Left Guard.

Yo mama's so nasty that she bit the dog and gave it rabies.

Yo mama's so nasty that she has a sign by her crotch that says: "Warning: May cause irritation, drowsiness, and a rash."

Yo mama's so nasty that she's got more clap than an auditorium.

Yo mama's so smelly, Bertie Bott made her his next jelly bean flavor.

Yo mama's breath is the secret ingredient in the Weasly's Butterscotch Barf-ies.

Yo mama's so stanky that not even Dobby would accept one of her socks.

Yo mama's breath is so nasty that it chases away Miasma.

Yo mama's so nasty that she calls Janet "Miss Jackson."

Yo mama's so nasty that she has more crabs then Red Lobster.

Yo mama's so nasty that next to her a skunk smells sweet.

Yo mama's so nasty that her poop is glad to escape her anus.

Yo mama's so nasty that when you were being delivered, the doctor was wearing an oxygen mask.

Yo mama's so nasty that every time she opens her mouth she's talking crap.

Yo mama's so nasty that even dogs won't sniff her crotch.

Yo mama's so nasty that the only dis I want to give her is a disinfectant.

Yo mama's so nasty that her crabs use her tampon string as a bungee cord.

Yo mama's so nasty that the original Order of the Phoenix was to "stay away from that woman!"

Yo mama's so nasty, the Forbidden Forest was named after her.

Yo mama's so nasty, every pair of her underwear has the Dark Mark on them.

YO MAMA'S SO STINKY...

Never expose her to an open flame.

It was easy to find yo mama when we played Hide-and-Seek. We just followed our noses.

Yo Mama's 3rd Grade Class

Yo mama's so stinky, she makes onions cry.

Yo mama's so stinky, she's Pigpen's idol.

Yo mama's so stinky, hogs run away from her.

Yo mama's so stinky, she sets off smog detectors.

Yo mama's so stinky, you can watch mildew growing on her back.

Yo mama's so stinky, she lives in the dump to hide her smell.

Yo mama's so stinky, Febreeze refuses to leave the squirt bottle.

Yo mama's so stinky, she can wilt a forest by taking a stroll.

Yo mama's so stinky, the flower shop pays her to avoid their street.

Yo mama's so stinky, the government uses her to deflect hurricanes.

Yo mama's so stinky, her high school nickname was Limburger.

Yo mama's so stinky, she's listed under "stinky" on Wikipedia.

Yo mama's so stinky, her armpits make her boobs throw up.

Yo mama's so stinky, her underwear hovers an inch away from touching her skin.

Yo mama's so stinky, she keeps vampires away better than garlic.

Yo mama's so stinky, she travels for free on merchant marine ships to keep Somalian pirates at bay.

Yo mama's so stinky, they use her to herd animals out of the rain forest.

Yo mama's so stinky, the government uses having her stand upwind as a military threat.

Yo mama's so stinky, the last time she went skinny-dipping was in the Sahara tropical jungle.

Yo mama's so stinky, she created the zombie apocalypse when the dead bodies in the graveyard next door got out of their graves to protest the stench.

Yo mama's so stinky, Voldemort calls her "she who must not be smelled."

Yo mama's so stinky, the cloud of stench around her can deflect the blast from the Death Star.

Yo Mama's So Short...

Hopefully she's not short-tempered...

Tell yo mama thanks for making me feel like a giant.

Napoleon

Yo mama's so short that you can see her feet on her driver's license!

Yo mama's so short that she has to use a ladder to pick up a dime.

Yo mama's so short that she does backflips under the bed.

Yo mama's so short that she models for trophys.

Yo mama's so short that her homies are the Keebler Elves.

Yo mama's so short that she has to get a running start to get up on the toilet.

Yo mama's so short that when she sneezes, she hits her head on the floor.

Yo mama's so short that she does pull-ups on a staple.

Yo mama's so short that she can do push-ups under the door.

Yo mama's so short that when I was dissin' her she tried to jump kick me in the ankle.

Yo mama's so short that she can limbo under the door.

Yo mama's so short that she uses a condom for a sleeping bag.

Yo mama's so short that she has to slam-dunk her bus fare.

Yo mama's so short that she has to look up to look down.

Yo mama's so short that she makes Gary Coleman look like Shaquille O'Neal.

Yo mama's so short, you can make a life size sculpture of her using one can of Play-Doh.

Yo mama's so short that when she sat on the curb her feet didn't touch the ground.

Yo mama's so short that she can play handball on the curb.

Yo mama's so short, politicians try to kiss her because they think she's a baby.

Yo mama's so short, she uses a doily as a skirt.

Yo mama's so short, she shops in the newborn clothes aisle.

Yo mama's so short, her underwear doubles as a t-shirt.

Yo mama's so short, she uses pinky rings as bracelets.

Yo mama's so short, if she wears dangly earrings they drag on the ground.

Yo mama's so short, she's the original old lady who lived in a shoe.

Yo mama's so short, she uses the Chihuahua as transportation.

Yo mama's so short, she keeps getting sucked up by the Roomba.

Yo mama's so short, she got her head stuck in a straw.

Yo mama's so short, it looks like her arms and legs are growing out of her butt.

Yo mama's so short, she has to jump on the keyboard to get it to print a character on the screen.

Yo mama's so short, these jokes go over her head.

Yo mama's so short, she has a 3-foot beehive hairdo to look normal.

Yo mama's so short, she's a plumber who cleans drains with a hammer and chisel.

Yo mama's so short, she keeps getting kidnapped by insect collectors.

YO MAMA'S SO TALL...

I heard she's head-and-shoulders above the rest...

Yes, I always looked up to my mama.

Shaquille O'Neal

Yo mama's so tall that she tripped in Michigan and bumped her head in Florida.

Yo mama's so tall that she tripped over a rock and hit her head on the moon.

Yo mama's so tall that if she did a back-flip she'd kick ET in the mouth.

Yo mama's so tall, she can see her house from anywhere.

Yo mama's so tall, she uses two 100-foot ladders as crutches.

Yo mama's so tall, she has to take out the driver's seat of her car and sit in the back to operate the vehicle.

Yo mama's so tall, she makes Shaquille O'Neal look like Gary Coleman.

Yo mama's so tall, she did a push-up and burned her back on the sun.

Yo mama's so tall, she uses a garden hose as a mini-skirt.

Yo mama's so tall, she was the one who got the baseball off of the roof without getting a ladder.

Yo mama's so tall, everyone can look up her skirt.

Yo mama's so tall, none of these jokes go over her head.

Yo mama's so tall, she puts the star on top of the Christmas tree without even stretching.

YO MAMA'S GLASSES ARE SO THICK...

So that's how she always knew what kind of trouble you were getting into when you were a kid...

I looked through two pairs of my mama's glasses and discovered the telescope.

Galileo

Yo mama's glasses are so thick, when she reads a map, she can see people waving.

Yo mama's glasses are so thick, she had to exercise her nose to hold them up.

Yo mama's glasses are so thick, they came with free tripods.

Yo mama's glasses are so thick, you can see the reflections from space.

Yo mama's glasses are so thick, when someone shone a laser through them they caused a volcano to erupt.

Yo mama's glasses are so thick, when she goes out in the sun she sets her face on fire.

Yo mama's glasses are so thick, she gets a Christmas card from the glasses manufacturer for keeping them in business.

Yo mama's glasses are so thick, her picture on her driver's license says "to be continued on the back."

Yo mama's glasses are so thick, her old set of glasses were repurposed as the sunroof of her car.

Yo mama's glasses are so thick, she ties balloons on them to hold them up.

Yo mama's glasses are so thick, Yoda uses them in the future in his lightsaber.

Yo mama's glasses are so thick, they bend light because of their gravity well.

Yo mama's glasses are so thick, she keeps banging them on the Eiffel Tower, even though she lives in Kansas.

Yo mama's glasses are so thick, she was banned from the hot air balloon festival when the morning sun shone through them and popped all the balloons.

Yo mama's glasses are so thick, it takes two months for light to pass through them.

Yo mama's glasses are so thick, they were made from Einstein-Bose condensate.

Yo mama's glasses are so thick, even Professor Flitwick couldn't make them fly with his *Wingardium Leviosa* spell.

Yo mama's glasses are so thick, even Dr. McCoy couldn't correct her vision.

Yo mama's glasses are so thick, even Professor Trelawny said, "Damn, your glasses are thick."

Yo mama's glasses are so thick, they used her prescription to double the power of the Hubble telescope.

YO MAMA'S SO GREASY...

I had to slide this chapter in...

Yo mama spent a summer here in the Middle-Eastern deserts. We've been extracting the oil now for decades.

Sheik Yerbooti

Yo mama's so greasy, she uses bacon as band-aids.

Yo mama's so greasy, she sweats Crisco.

Yo mama's so greasy, she wrings her sheets for cooking oil.

Yo mama's so greasy, Texaco buys the oil that drips off of her.

Yo mama's so greasy that she sweats butter and syrup and has a full time job at Denny's wiping pancakes across her forehead.

Yo mama's so greasy that her freckles slipped off.

Yo mama's so greasy that if Crisco had a football team, she'd be the mascot.

Yo mama's so greasy that she squeezes Crisco from her hair to bake cookies.

Yo mama's so greasy that she's labeled as an ingredient in Crisco.

Yo mama's so greasy that her face could free the U.S. from its dependence on foreign oil.

Yo mama's so greasy that you could fry a chicken dinner for 12 on her forehead.

Yo mama's so greasy that I buttered my popcorn with her leg hairs.

Yo mama's so greasy makeup drips off within seconds.

Yo mama's so greasy she fills the tank in her diesel truck with her nose drippings.

Yo mama's so greasy she drips vinegar on her face to make salad dressing.

Yo mama's so greasy she can limbo under closed doors.

Yo mama's so greasy you can fry eggs and hash browns on her stomach when she's sun bathing.

Yo mama's so greasy, I got burned by splattering oil when the sun shone on her face.

Yo mama's so greasy KFC thought she was smuggling their cooking oil in her hair.

Yo mama's so greasy she makes whole cornfields pop when she drives through Kansas.

Yo mama's so greasy she takes a shower at the local car wash.

Yo mama's so greasy she leaves an oil slick in the ocean when she goes swimming.

Yo mama's so greasy, she accidentally set her face on fire and it's been burning for over seventeen years.

Yo mama's so greasy Voldemort's *Avada Kedavra* spell just slides off.

Yo mama's so greasy the Tin Man dated her to keep himself properly oiled.

YO MAMA'S SO POOR...

Donations accepted via PayPal

No matter how bad things are – our house gone from the tornado, the car swallowed by a volcano, our clothes made out of Walmart bags – at least we're not as bad off as yo mama.

Auntie M, from the Wizard of Oz

Yo mama's so poor, she goes to KFC and licks other people's fingers.

Yo mama's so poor, when I rang the doorbell she yelled "DING DONG!"

Yo mama's so poor, she eats Costco free food samples for dinner.

Yo mama's so poor, she ran outside with a bag when she heard there was a change in the weather.

Yo mama's so poor, she went to McDonald's and put a milkshake on layaway.

Yo mama's so poor, burglars leave stuff behind in pity.

Yo mama's so poor, even Republicans want to give her welfare.

Yo mama's so poor, she hangs out toilet paper to dry.

Yo mama's so poor, she wrestled a squirrel for a peanut.

Yo mama's so poor, I stepped in through the front door and fell out the back.

Yo mama's so poor, when I saw her walking down the street with one shoe and asked, "You lose a shoe?" she replied, "No, found one."

Yo mama's so poor, she hangs Jiffy Pop from the roof instead of a fire detector.

Yo mama's so poor, she eats cereal with a fork to save milk.

Yo mama's so poor, people rob her house just for the practice.

Yo mama's so poor, her face is on the front of a food stamp.

Yo mama's so poor that she was in K-Mart with a box of Hefty bags and when I asked her what she was doing, she said, "Buying luggage."

Yo mama's so poor that she can't afford to pay attention!

Yo mama's so poor that when I saw her kicking a can down the street, I asked her what she was doing, and she said "moving."

Yo mama's so poor that she waves around a Popsicle stick and calls it air conditioning.

Yo mama's so poor that I saw her running after a garbage truck with a shopping list.

Yo mama's so poor that the bank repossesed her cardboard box.

Yo mama's so poor Nigerian scammers wire HER money!

Yo mama's so poor she couldn't afford to apply for Medicare!

Yo mama's so poor that she has to wear her McDonald's uniform to church.

Yo mama's so poor that she's got more furniture on her porch than in her house.

Yo mama's so poor that I came over for dinner and she read me recipes.

Yo mama's so poor that she has to take the trash IN.

Yo mama's so poor that she had to get a second mortgage on her cardboard box.

Yo mama's so poor that she lives in a two story Dorito bag with a dog named Chip.

Yo mama's so poor that her front and back doors are on the same hinge.

Yo mama's so poor that the closest thing to a car she has is a low-rider shopping cart with a box on it.

Yo mama's so poor that she can't even put her two cents in this conversation.

Yo mama's so poor that I went to her house and tore down some cob webs, and she said "Who's tearing down the drapes?"

Yo mama's so poor that I stepped on her skateboard and she said "Hey, get off the car!"

Yo mama's so poor that I walked into her house, asked to use the bathroom, and she said "3rd bucket to your right."

Yo mama's so poor that when I walked inside her house and put out a cigarette, she said "who turned off the heater?"

Yo mama's so poor that your TV got 2 channels: ON and OFF.

Yo mama's so poor that she watches TV on an Etch-A-Sketch.

Yo mama's so poor that she can't even afford to go to the free clinic.

Yo mama's so poor that she washes paper plates.

Yo mama's so poor that her idea of a fortune cookie is a tortilla with a food stamp in it.

Yo mama's so poor that when your family watches TV, they go to Sears.

Yo mama's so poor that burglars break in and leave money.

Yo mama's so poor that she married young just to get the rice!

Yo mama's so poor that when I went over to her house for dinner and grabbed a paper plate, she said "Don't use the good china!"

Yo mama's so poor that when I saw her rolling some trash cans around in an alley, I asked her what she was doing, she said "Remodeling."

Yo mama's so poor that I threw a rock at a trash can and she popped out and said "Who knocked?"

Yo mama's so poor that when we were on a road trip and she stopped by a dumpster and got out, I asked what she was doing and she replied, "I booked a hotel!"

Yo mama's so poor that I walked into her house and swatted a firefly and Yo Mama said, "Who turned off the lights?"

Yo mama's so poor that when I asked what was for dinner, she pulled her shoelaces off and said "Spaghetti."

Yo Mama's so poor she can't even afford a Gringotts account.

Yo mama's so poor that Dobby gave her a sock to keep her foot warm.

Yo mama's so poor she had to go to the Weasley's for a loan.

Yo mama's so poor that after I pissed in your yard, she thanked me for watering the lawn.

Yo mama's so poor that she got in an elevator and thought it was a mobile home.

Yo mama's so poor that for Halloween, she stole all of the treats.

Yo mama's so poor that when she tells people her address, she says "it's in the second alley from Main Street, beside the yellow dumpster."

Yo mama's so poor that her idea of a timeshare is a few days camped out under a bridge.

Yo mama's so poor that when I saw her in the park digging up plants, she said she was "getting groceries".

Yo mama's so poor that when I ring the doorbell I hear the toilet flush!

Yo mama's so poor, she hid under a bridge and tried to eat the Three Billy Goats Gruff.

Yo mama's so poor, her idea of a bank is jumping in a wishing well.

Yo mama's so poor, she eats corn from hospital bedpans.

Yo mama's so poor, Klingons took pity on her.

Yo mama's so poor, she brings home leftovers from her job in the morgue.

Yo mama's so poor, she wears gowns made of Walmart bags.

Yo mama's so poor, she orders hot water at a restaurant and makes soup out of the ketchup.

Yo Mama's So Lazy...

I'll write something here later...maybe...

I got my laziness from my mama. I didn't want to call my wife in the kitchen to bring me a beer, so I invented the telephone.

Alexander Graham Bell

Yo mama's so lazy, she thinks a two-income family is where the husband has two full-time jobs.

Yo mama's so lazy, she got a remote control for her remote.

Yo mama's so lazy, she had you so you could change the channel for her.

Yo mama's so lazy, her metal chair has a bundentation.

Yo mama's so lazy, she snacks on mushrooms that grow on her couch.

Yo mama's so lazy, she shortened her name to Ma.

Yo mama's so lazy, she got a sleeper sofa so she could sit and sleep without ever getting up.

Yo mama's so lazy, she wears seven pairs of underwear at a time so she doesn't have to change her clothes all week.

Yo mama's so lazy, she has you chew her food and spit it in her mouth.

Yo mama's so lazy, she set up a drive thru lane next to her couch so the pizza man could deliver without her getting up.

Yo mama's so lazy, she sits on a Slip-n-Slide so she doesn't have to get up to go to the bathroom.

Yo mama's so lazy, she sets off the fire sprinklers to take a shower.

Yo mama's so lazy, birds poop on her because they think she's a statue.

Yo mama's so lazy, she was elected to the US Senate.

Yo mama's so lazy, she installed a conveyor belt to deliver food from the kitchen.

Yo mama's so lazy, she went golfing and is still stuck on the first hole, eight years later.

Yo mama's so lazy, she had a second child to watch the first one.

Yo mama's so lazy, she uses spray paint to apply makeup.

Yo mama's so lazy, she puts coffee grounds in her mustache and drinks hot water.

Yo mama's so lazy, she didn't do enough to fill up this chapter.

Yo Mama's So Fat...

Oddly enough, this is one of the biggest chapters.

People say I'm too overweight; that I'm not in shape. Well, round is a shape.

Roseanne Barr

Yo mama's so fat, when her beeper goes off people think she's backing up.

Yo mama's so fat, her nickname is "Lardo".

Yo mama's so fat, she eats Wheat Thicks.

Yo mama's so fat, we're in her right now.

Yo mama's so fat, people jog around her for exercise.

Yo mama's so fat, she went to the movies and sat next to everyone.

Yo mama's so fat, she's been declared a natural habitat for condors.

Yo mama's so fat, she lays on the beach and people run around yelling "Free Willy!"

Yo mama's so fat, when she wants someone to shake her hand she has to give directions.

Yo mama's so fat, she goes to a restaurant, looks at the menu, and says, "OK."

Yo mama's so fat, when she wears a yellow raincoat, people yell, "Taxi!"

Yo mama's so fat, she had to go to Sea World to get baptized.

Yo mama's so fat, she has to iron her pants in the driveway.

Yo mama's so fat, she puts her makeup on with a paint roller.

Yo mama's so fat, when she bungee jumps, she brings down the whole bridge.

Yo mama's so fat, the highway patrol makes her wear a "wide load" sign on her butt.

Yo mama's so fat, when she sits around the house, she sits AROUND THE HOUSE.

Yo mama's so fat, when she gets on the scale, it screams in agony.

Yo mama's so fat, when she gets on a scale, it says, "One at a time, please."

Yo mama's so fat, when she steps on a scale, it explodes.

Yo mama's so fat, when she steps on a scale, the dial goes around so fast she goes back in time.

Yo mama's so fat, when she steps on a scale, it says, "To be continued..."

Yo mama's so fat, she fell in love and broke it.

Yo mama's so fat, she has her own zip code.

Yo mama's so fat, she has her own area code.

Yo mama's so fat, she has her own time zone.

Yo mama's so fat, she was accused of smuggling a Volkswagen from the dealer.

Yo mama's so fat, when she goes to the beach, the tide comes in.

Yo mama's so fat, when she goes to the beach, shellfish swim for their lives.

Yo mama's so fat, when she goes to the beach, the sand under her feet turns to glass from the pressure.

Yo mama's so fat, when she goes to the beach, the ocean doubles in size from the sweat in her fat folds.

Yo mama's so fat, when she goes to the beach, Greenpeace tries to roll her back into the ocean.

Yo mama's so fat, even Bill Gates couldn't afford her liposuction.

Yo mama's so fat, I had to take two buses and a train just to get on her good side.

Yo mama's so fat, she wakes up in sections.

Yo mama's so fat, she rolled over four quarters and it turned into a dollar.

Yo mama's so fat, when she goes to the beach, no one else gets any sun.

Yo mama's so fat, when she jumps up in the air, she gets stuck.

Yo mama's so fat, her senior pictures were aerial shots.

Yo mama's so fat, she's on both sides of the family.

Yo mama's so fat, she has to use a boomerang to put on a belt.

Yo mama's so fat, when she crosses the street, cars look out for her.

Yo mama's so fat, the photographer has to take fifty steps back just to get her full head in the picture.

Yo mama's so fat, when she walks, she makes the CDs skip at the radio station.

Yo mama's so fat, she's twice the man as your father.

Yo mama's so fat, elephants throw peanuts at her.

Yo mama's so fat, "Place your Ad Here" is printed on her back.

Yo mama's so fat, the circus tent manufacturer makes her t-shirts.

Yo mama's so fat, when she wears heels, they're flats by the afternoon.

Yo mama's so fat, when she leaves the beach everyone yells, "The coast is clear!"

Yo mama's so fat, whenever she wears high heels, she strikes oil.

Yo mama's so fat, she fell and made the Grand Canyon.

Yo mama's so fat, when she broke her leg, gravy came out.

Yo mama's so fat, they had to grease the bathtub to get her out.

Yo mama's so fat, she had to be registered with the DMV.

Yo mama's so fat that China uses her to block the internet.

Yo mama $= x/0$ for every x in yo mama.

The infinite series of yo mama from 0 to infinity is strictly diverging.

Yo mama's so fat that NASA shot a rocket into her butt looking for water.

Yo mama's so fat that she doesn't just have a low center of gravity, she has an elliptical orbit.

Yo mama's so fat that IEEE is working on a wifi protocol so people can get the signals to reach users on opposite sides of her. It's called 802.11 Draft Fat Mama.

If we were to code your mom in a C++ function she would look like this: double mom (double fat){ mom(fat);return mom;}; //your mom is recursively fat.

Yo mama's so big that she has a gravitational pull equal to that of the sun.

Yo mama's so big that doctors use scuba divers as nanobots to clean her arteries.

The mass of yo mama at rest is approximately equal to that of a neutron star traveling at $(1-(10^{-1000}))c$.

Yo mama's so fat that she and the Great Wall of China are used as reference points when astronauts look back at the Earth.

Yo mama's so fat that she has to use the truck scales.

Yo mama's so round that she makes a Pokéball look flat!

Yo mama's like a converging lens - she's wider in the middle than she is on either end.

Yo mama's a convenient proof that the universe is still expanding exponentially.

Yo mama's so fat, they use the elastic in her underwear for bungee jumping.

Yo mama's so fat, when she fell over, she rocked herself to sleep trying to get up again.

Yo mama's so fat, when I tried to drive around her I ran out of gas.

Yo mama's so fat, when she dances at a concert, the music skips.

Yo mama's so fat, you have to grease the door frame and hold out a Twinkie on the other side just to get her through.

Yo mama's so fat, she sets off car alarms when she walks by.

Yo mama's so fat, she hula-hoops with the super bowl.

Yo mama's so fat, she shows up on radar.

Yo mama's so fat, she thinks a balanced meal is a whole ham in each hand.

Yo mama's so fat, she programs in C++++++++.

Yo mama's so fat, she got flesh-eating disease and the doctor gave her 40 years to live.

Yo mama's so fat, she was rezoned for commercial development.

Yo mama's so fat, her polo shirt has a real horse on it.

Yo mama's so fat, when she sits down, chairs beg for mercy.

Yo mama's so fat, when she gets up, she has to fluff metal chairs.

Yo mama's so fat, she gets group rates at restaurants.

Yo mama's so fat, she's taller when she lies down.

Yo mama's so fat, your father had to have a sherpa to guide him to get on top of her.

Yo mama's so fat, the last time she saw 90210 was on a scale.

Yo mama's so fat, the only thing stopping her from going to Jenny Craig is the width of the door.

Yo mama's so fat, when she auditioned for a role in Indiana Jones she got the part of the boulder.

Yo mama's so fat, her face covered all sides of the milk carton when she was kidnapped.

Yo mama's so fat, she whistles bass.

Yo mama's so fat, when she goes to a restaurant, she doesn't get a menu—she gets an estimate.

Yo mama's so fat, when she takes a shower, her feet don't get wet.

Yo mama's so fat, when she was born, instead of a birth certificate she got blueprints.

Yo mama's so fat, when she goes to a parade everyone assumes she's a float.

Yo mama's so fat, she tripped in Michigan and knocked Florida into the ocean.

Yo mama's so fat, her mattress cries at night.

Yo mama's so fat, they had to change "one size fits all" to "one size fits most".

Yo mama's so fat, when she tripped her butt got tanned from the reentry.

Yo mama's so fat, even her shadow has stretch marks.

Yo mama's so fat, her belly button doesn't have lint, it has whole sweaters.

Yo mama's so fat, her belly button has an echo.

Yo mama's so fat, if she weighed five more pounds she could get a group rate on insurance.

Yo mama's so fat, my dog bit her and died from high cholesterol.

Yo mama's so fat, NASA has satellites orbiting her.

Yo mama's so fat, she trick or treats one whole block at a time.

Yo mama's so fat, she won first, second, and third place at a pie-eating contest.

Yo mama's so fat, she had her baby pictures taken by satellite.

Yo mama's so fat, she had her ears pierced with a harpoon.

Yo mama's so fat, she had to roll over nine times to get an even tan.

Yo mama's so fat, she has to keep pesos in one pocket and yen in the other.

Yo mama's so fat, she wears a six-piece bathing suit.

Yo mama's so fat, she leaves stretch marks on the bathtub.

Yo mama's so fat, she makes Jabba the Hutt look anorexic.

Yo mama's so fat, she eats cereal out of the super bowl.

Yo mama's so fat, when she stands in the left turn lane it gives her a green arrow.

Yo mama's so fat, when she was born, she gave the hospital stretch marks.

Yo mama's so fat that her bellybutton gets home 15 minutes before she does.

Yo mama's so fat that the National Weather Service names each one of her farts.

Yo mama's so fat and dumb that the only reason she opened her email was because she heard it contained spam.

Yo mama's so fat she threw on a sheet for Halloween and went as Antarctica.

Yo mama's so fat that she looked up cheat codes for Wii Fit.

Yo mama's so fat that the only exercise she gets is when she chases the ice cream truck.

Yo mama's so fat that she sat on a dollar and squeezed a booger out George Washington's nose.

Yo mama's so fat that when she gets in an elevator, it has to go down.

Yo mama's so fat that she left the house in high heels and came back wearing flip flops.

Yo mama's so fat that she was floating in the ocean and Spain claimed her for the New World.

Yo mama's so fat that when she walked in front of the TV, I missed 3 seasons of Breaking Bad.

Yo mama's so fat that when she talks to herself, it's a long distance call.

Yo mama's so fat that light bends around her.

Yo mama's so fat that I took a picture of her last Christmas and it's still printing!

Yo mama's so fat that when she sat on Wal-Mart, she lowered the prices.

Yo mama's so fat that when she sat on an iPhone, it turned into an iPod.

Yo mama's so fat that even prayer can't lift her spirit.

Yo mama's so fat that she walked into the Gap and filled it.

Yo mama's so fat that she comes at you from all directions.

Yo mama's so fat that when she climbed onto a diving board at the beach, the lifeguard told your dad "sorry, you can't park here".

Yo mama's so fat that her cereal bowl came with a lifeguard.

Yo mama's so fat that when she got her shoes shined, she had to take the guy's word for it.

Yo mama's so fat that when she sings, it's over for everybody.

Yo mama's so fat that when she was growing up she didn't play with dolls, she played with midgets.

Yo mama's so fat that she uses two buses for roller-blades.

Yo mama's so fat she blew up the Deathstar.

Yo mama's so fat that when she goes to a buffet, she gets the group rate.

Yo mama's so fat that she broke the Stairway to Heaven.

Yo mama's so fat that she doesn't eat with a fork, she eats with a forklift.

Yo mama's so fat that the last time the landlord saw her, he doubled the rent.

Yo mama's so fat that Weight Watchers won't look at her.

Yo mama's so fat that she fell in love and broke it.

Yo mama's so fat that when she gets on the scale it says "We don't do livestock".

Yo mama's so fat that when she tripped on 4th Ave, she landed on 12th.

Yo mama's so fat that God couldn't light the Earth until she moved!

Yo mama's so fat that when she goes to a buffet, it goes out of business.

Yo mama's so fat that she has to pull down her pants to get into her pockets.

Yo mama's so fat that she was born on the fourth, fifth, and sixth of June.

Yo mama's so fat that she could fall down and wouldn't even know it.

Yo mama's so fat that the sign inside one restaurant says, "Maximum occupancy: 300, or Yo Mama."

Yo mama's so fat that she puts mayonnaise on aspirin.

Yo mama's so fat that she was born with a silver shovel in her mouth.

Yo mama's so fat that when she hauls ass, she has to make two trips.

Yo mama's so fat that when she turns around people throw her a welcome back party.

Yo mama's so fat that a picture of her would fall off the wall.

Yo mama's so fat that she could sell shade.

Yo mama's so fat that I ran around her twice and got lost.

Yo mama's so fat that the shadow of her butt weighs 100 pounds.

Yo mama's so fat that when she's standing on the corner police drive by and yell, "Hey, break it up."

Yo mama's so fat that her blood type is Ragu.

Yo mama's so fat that when she runs the fifty-yard dash she needs an overnight bag.

Yo mama's so fat that she can't even fit into a chat room.

Yo mama's so fat when she goes skydiving she doesn't use a parachute to land, she uses a twin-engine plane!

Yo mama's so fat MTX audio's subwoofers couldn't rattle her bones!

Yo mama's so fat her headphones are a pair of PA speakers connected to a car amplifier.

Yo mama's so fat that she doesn't have a tailor, she has a contractor.

Yo mama's so fat that eating contests have banned her because she is unfair competition.

Yo mama's so fat that she measures 36-24-36, and the other arm is just as big.

Yo mama's so fat that she gets her toenails painted at Lucky's Auto Body.

Yo mama's so fat that when she goes to an amusement park, people try to ride HER!

Yo mama's so fat that when she jumps up in the air she gets stuck!

Yo mama's so fat that she influences the tides.

Yo mama's so fat that when she plays hopscotch, she goes "New York, L.A., Chicago..."

Yo mama's so fat that when she sits on my face I can't hear the stereo.

Yo mama's so fat you have to roll over twice to get off her.

Yo mama's so fat that she sets off car alarms when she runs.

Yo mama's so fat that she can't reach into her back pocket.

Yo mama's so fat that she has her own gravity field.

Yo mama's so fat that she stepped on a rainbow and made Skittles.

Yo mama's so fat that when she wears a "Malcolm X" T-shirt, helicopters try to land on her back!

Yo mama's so fat that that she can't tie her own shoes.

Yo mama's so fat that she uses redwoods to pick her teeth.

Yo mama's so fat that she went on a light diet. As soon as it's light she starts eating.

Yo mama's so fat that she's half Italian, half Irish, and half American.

Yo mama's so fat that her waist size is the Equator.

Yo mama's so fat that she can't even jump to a conclusion.

Yo mama's so fat that she uses a mattress for a tampon.

Yo mama's so fat that when she got hit by a bus, she said, "Who threw that rock at me?"

Yo mama's so fat that we went to the drive-in and didn't have to pay for her because we dressed her up as a Toyota.

Yo mama's so fat that she was cut from the cast of E.T., because she caused an eclipse when she rode the bike across the moon.

Yo mama's so fat that when you get on top of her your ears pop.

Yo mama's so fat that she got hit by a car and had to go to the hospital to have it removed.

Yo mama's so fat that even Dora can't explore her!

Yo mama's so fat that even Chuck Norris couldn't run around her.

Yo mama's so fat that her neck looks like a dozen hot dogs!

Yo mama's so fat that when she bungee jumps she goes straight to hell!

Yo mama's so fat that she has to buy three airline tickets.

Yo mama's so fat that she's got Amtrak written on her leg.

Yo mama's so fat that her legs are like spoiled milk - white & chunky!

Yo mama's so fat that she wakes up in sections!

Yo mama's so fat that her butt drags on the ground and kids yell - "there goes Santa Claus with his bag of toys!"

Yo mama's so fat that even her clothes have stretch marks!

Yo mama's so fat that she has to use a VCR as a beeper!

Yo mama's so fat that when she asked for a waterbed, they put a blanket over the ocean!

Yo mama's so fat that she got hit by a parked car!

Yo mama's so fat that when we were playing Call of Duty, I got a 20 kill streak for killing her.

Yo mama's so fat that Dracula got Type 2 Diabetes after biting her neck.

Yo mama's so fat that when she went to church and sat on a bible, Jesus came out and said "LET MY PEOPLE GO!"

Yo mama's so fat that she went to the fair and the kids thought she was a bouncy castle.

Yo mama's so fat that when she goes to an all you can eat buffet, they have to install speed bumps.

Yo mama's so fat that her sedan can fit 5 people... or just yo mama with the front seats removed.

Yo mama's so fat that when she went to SeaWorld the whales started singing "We Are Family".

Yo mama's so fat that she fell out of both sides of her bed.

Yo mama's so fat that the stripes on her pajamas never end.

Yo mama's so fat, Al Gore accuses her of global warming every time she farts!

Yo mama's so fat that she's got every caterer in the city on speed dial!

Yo mama's so fat that when she goes on a scale, it shows her own phone number.

Yo mama's so fat that she doesn't need the Internet— she's worldwide.

Yo mama's so fat that when she goes on a scale, it reads "lose some weight".

Yo mama's so fat that she doesn't get dreams, she gets movies!

Yo mama's so fat that when she walks, she changes the earth's rotation!

Yo mama's so fat that she uses the entire country of Mexico as her tanning bed.

Yo mama's so fat that the Sorting Hat put her in all four houses!

Yo mama's so fat that a *Wingardium Leviosa* spell couldn't lift her.

Yo mama's so fat, she makes Hagrid look like "Mini-me".

Yo mama's so fat, she tried to eat Cornelius Fudge.

Yo mama's so fat the Sorting Hat assigned her to the House of Pancakes.

Yo Mama's so fat, her Patronus is a Double-Whopper with Cheese.

Yo mama's so fat, she used the invisibility cloak as a bib.

Yo mama's so fat that even the Dementors can't suck her soul out in one sitting.

Yo mama's so fat, she looked in the Mirror of Erised and saw a ham!

Yo mama's so fat that if she confronted a boggart it would morph into a treadmill.

Yo mama's so fat that the Sorting Hat couldn't decide where to put her - she couldn't fit in any of the houses!!

Yo mama's so fat, she ate the Death Eaters.

Yo mama's so fat even Grawp can't pick her up!

Yo mama's so fat that it takes eleven boggarts to shape-shift into her!

Yo mama's so fat that even her Quidditch robes have stretch marks.

Yo mama's so fat they'd have to use transfiguration to sneak her through the hole in the Gryffindor Tower.

Ya mama's so fat, her wand is a Slim Jim.

Yo mama's so fat the core of her wand has a cream filling.

Yo mama's so fat that a $700 billion bailout would only keep her fed for a week.

Yo mama's so fat that the housing bubble popped because she sat on it!

Yo mama's so fat that she supported the bailout just because she wanted a 'barrel of pork'.

Yo mama's so fat that even Mitt Romney couldn't afford to take her out to dinner!

Yo mama's so fat that her biography is called "The Audacity of Hardee's".

Yo mama's so fat that Sarah Palin can see her from her house.

Yo mama's so fat that Sarah Palin can't see Russia anymore!.

Yo mama's so fat that "ACORN" registered her to vote eight times!

Yo mama's so fat that even the Death Star couldn't blow her up!

Yo mama's so fat that Spock couldn't find a pressure point to perform the Vulcan Death Grip on her.

Yo mama's so fat the odds against not finding her fat are approximately 3,720 to 1.

Yo mama's so fat that she thought the opening line of Kirk's monologue was "Spice, the final Frontier..."

Yo mama's so fat that if she were placed beside a changeling during regeneration, no one would know the difference.

Yo mama's so fat that she tried to fly through a temporal anomaly but she didn't fit.

Yo mama's so fat she makes Riker's belly look 3 atoms thick.

Yo mama's so fat that when she tried to captain a Galaxy Class starship they had to separate the saucer so she could fit.

Yo mama's so fat that she makes the USS Enterprise look like a micro machines racer.

Yo mama's so fat that only half her body was able to come out frozen from the carbon freezing chamber in Cloud City.

Guy A. De Marco

Yo mama's so fat that when she beams to a ship, the ship beams inside of her.

Yo mama's so fat that the passengers of the Millenium Falcon mistook her for a small moon.

Yo mama's so fat that Gardulla the Hutt had a boost in self-esteem after seeing her.

Yo mama's so fat that she fell to the dark side and couldn't get back up.

Yo mama's so fat that if she was thrown into the second Death Star's reactor core, she could have blown up the entire Imperial fleet.

Yo mama's so fat that the Kaminoans couldn't use her as a host for clones since they couldn't pierce her skin deep enough to draw blood.

Yo mama's so fat that she caused Kamino to flood when her water broke.

Yo mama's so fat that her lack of balance caused her to stumble into an Utapau sinkhole.

Yo Mama's so fat, that in an attempt to beam her up, the ship ended up being pulled down to the surface.

Yo Mama's so fat that when she walks into a room the replicators stop working.

Yo Mama's so fat, Data feels strong emotions of disgust and self-terminates.

Yo Mama's so fat she wears her own inertia dampener.

Yo Mama's so fat, she managed to contain a warp core breach.

Yo Mama's so fat, she got stuck trying to enter the Nexus.

Yo Mama's so fat, when she fell over, she punched a hole in the fabric of space/time.

Yo mama's so fat that she took geometry in high school just cause she heard there was some pi.

Yo mama's so fat that the ratio of the circumference to her diameter is four.

Yo mama's so fat that in a love triangle, she'd be the hypotenuse.

The integral of Yo mama's fat plus a constant, where the constant is equal to more fat.

Yo mama's muscle-to-fat ratio can only be explained in irrational complex numbers.

The only way to get from point A to point B is around yo mama's fat butt.

Yo mama's so fat that her derivative is strictly positive.

The volume of Yo mama's an improper integral.

The limit of yo mama's ass goes to infinity.

Yo mama's so fat that she expresses her weight in scientific notation.

Yo mama's so fat that scientists track her position by observing anomalies in Pluto's orbit.

Yo mama's so fat that a recursive function computing her weight causes a stack overflow.

Yo mama's so fat that the long double numeric variable type in C++ is insufficient to express her weight.

Yo mama's so fat that THX can't even surround her.

Yo Mama's so fat, she walked in front of the TV and I missed three seasons of Inuyasha!

Yo mama's so fat, Naruto couldnt make enough clones to see all sides of her.

Yo mama's so fat that the Dragon Ball Z crew uses her to make craters on set.

Yo mama's so fat that when she sat down on a park bench, she caused the Naruto timeskip.

Yo mama's so fat, she scared L into giving up all sweets.

Yo mama's so fat that she can't even fit in the expanding plug suit.

Yo mama's so fat that she broke the HP limit!

Yo mama's so fat, she makes Vash look anorexic!

Yo mama's so fat that she was mistaken for Mt. Fuji at the Sakura festival.

Yo mama's so fat she makes a Snorlax look like a Chihuahua!

Yo mama's so fat that it took the entire Dragon Ball Z crew 1 week just to lift her off the ground.

Yo mama's so fat that she tried to eat someone dressed as a box of Pocky!

Yo mama's so fat, Choji told her to lose weight.

Yo mama's so fat, she makes Harry Potter's Aunt Marge look like a stick figure.

YO MAMA'S SO DUMB...

This subtitle is in French when you're not looking.

Bill Clinton said he hid a hundred dollars in the corner of the oval office. I wore out the knees of my jeans trying to find it.

Monica Lewinsky

Yo mama's so stupid, when she saw the NC-17 rating at the movies, she went home and brought along 16 friends.

Yo mama's so stupid, when your dad said it was chilly out, she ran outside with a spoon.

Yo mama's so stupid, she puts lipstick on the top of her head just to make up her mind.

Yo mama's so stupid, you have to dig for her I.Q.

Yo mama's so stupid, she got locked in a grocery store and starved.

Yo mama's so stupid, she tried to put M&M's in alphabetical order.

Yo mama's so stupid, she was fired from the M&M factory for rejecting the W's.

Yo mama's so stupid, she sold her car for gas money.

Yo mama's so stupid, she thinks a quarterback is a refund.

Yo mama's so stupid, she got a job in a tree house because she wanted to be a branch manager.

Yo mama's so stupid, she saw her reflection in the TV and thought she was on Jeopardy.

Yo mama's so stupid, she puts stamps on her faxes.

Yo mama's so stupid, she sold her camera to buy film.

Yo mama's so stupid, she tried to buy film for her digital camera.

Yo mama's so stupid, she thinks "stereotype" is a brand of radio.

Yo mama's so stupid, she thinks Tiger Woods is a forest in India.

Yo mama's so stupid, she thinks a lawsuit is something you wear to court.

Yo mama's so stupid, she thinks Meow Mix is music for cats.

Yo mama's so stupid, she thinks Thailand is a mens clothing store.

Yo mama's so stupid, she told me to meet her on the corner of Walk and Don't Walk.

Yo mama's so stupid, she went to the drive-in theater to see "Closed for the Season."

Yo mama's so stupid, she tried to commit suicide by jumping out of the basement window.

Yo mama's so stupid, when the judge said, "Order!" she said "Fries and a coke, please."

Yo mama's so stupid, she tried to steal a free sample.

Yo mama's so stupid, she dials 911 on the microwave.

Yo mama's so stupid, when she got pregnant, she asked, "Is it mine?"

Yo mama's so stupid, she called the operator to get the phone number for 911.

Yo mama's so stupid, she took a ruler to bed to see how long she slept.

Yo mama's so stupid, when she saw a note on a form that said not to write below the dotted line, she wrote, "OK."

Yo mama's so stupid, she took a spoon to the Superbowl.

Yo mama's so stupid, if you put your ear next to hers you hear the ocean.

Yo mama's so stupid, when I told her to buy a color TV, she asked, "What color?"

Yo mama's so stupid, she stayed at a stop sign waiting for it to say "go".

Yo mama's so stupid, she needs twice her IQ to be classified as a half-wit.

Yo mama's so stupid, she uses correction fluid on her computer monitor to fix mistakes.

Yo mama's so stupid, she gets confused when the computer says, "press any key to continue."

Yo mama's so stupid, she stared at an orange juice box because it said, "concentrate."

Yo mama's so stupid, she stands on the corner with a sign saying, "will eat for food!"

Yo mama's so stupid, she got in an elevator and thought it was a mobile home.

Yo mama's so stupid, she saw a billboard that said "Dodge Trucks", so she started slaloming through traffic.

Yo mama's so stupid, she got locked in a car—and it was a convertible with the top down.

Yo mama's so stupid, she studied for a blood test.

Yo mama's so stupid, she failed the census.

Yo mama's so stupid, she asks for price checks at the dollar store.

Yo mama's so stupid, she bought a silent car alarm.

Yo mama's so stupid, on her job application, where it said "sign here", she put Sagittarius."

Yo mama's so stupid, her brain cells are on the endangered species list.

Yo mama's so stupid, her latest invention was a glass hammer.

Yo mama's so stupid, her shoes say "TGIF" for "Toes Go in First."

Yo mama's so stupid, she learned the running man dance move and I haven't seen her since.

Yo mama's so stupid, when she heard Christmas was just around the corner, she went looking for it.

Yo mama's so stupid, when I said I was reading a book by Homer, she asked if I had anything written by Bart.

Yo mama's so stupid, if brains were dynamite she couldn't blow her nose.

Yo mama's so stupid, it takes her an hour to cook minute rice.

Yo mama's so stupid, when her job application asked for an emergency contact, she put "911"

Yo mama's so stupid, she got a refund for a jigsaw puzzle because she thought it was broken.

Yo mama's so stupid, she returned a donut to the bakery because it had a hole in it.

Yo mama's so stupid, she can't pass a sobriety test when she's sober.

Yo mama's so stupid, she climbed over a chain link fence to see what was on the other side.

Yo mama's so stupid, she cooked her own complimentary breakfast.

Yo mama's so stupid, she cooks with Old Spice.

Yo mama's so stupid, she tried to read an audiobook.

Yo mama's so stupid, she died before the police arrived because she couldn't find the eleven key when dialing 911.

Yo mama's so stupid, she was hit by a coffee cup and told the cops she was mugged.

Yo mama's so stupid, she took a coffee cup to get her mug shot taken.

Yo mama's so stupid, she got locked in the bathroom and wet her pants.

Yo mama's so stupid, she got locked in a mattress store and slept on the floor.

Yo mama's so stupid, she invented a wheelchair with pedals.

Yo mama's so stupid, she tried to deposit her watch at the bank to save time.

Yo mama's so stupid, she studied for a urine test.

Yo mama's so stupid, she thought Taco Bell was the Mexican phone company.

Yo mama's so stupid, she thought Fleetwood Mac was a new specialty burger at McDonald's.

Yo mama's so stupid, she sits on the TV and watches the couch.

Yo mama's so stupid, she thought Boys II Men was a day care center.

Yo mama's so stupid, she bought a video camera to record cable TV shows at home.

Yo mama's so stupid, instead of taking the route 44 bus, she rode the 22 bus twice.

Yo mama's so stupid, under Education on her job application, she put, "Hooked on Phonics."

Yo mama's so stupid, when she watches the Three Stooges, she takes notes.

Yo mama's so slow and dumb that she can be emulated on a 286.

Yo mama's dumber than an augmented rat.

Yo mama's so stupid that her exchange particle is a "moron".

Yo mama's so dumb that she went to the dentist and asked for a bluetooth.

Yo mama's so stupid that when I told her *pi-r-squared*, she replied no, they are round.

Yo mama's so stupid that it took her 2 hours to watch 60 Minutes!

Yo mama's so stupid that when she went for a blood test, she asked for time to study.

Yo mama's so stupid that she tripped over a cordless phone!

Yo mama's so stupid that she told everyone that she was "illegitimate" because she couldn't read.

Yo mama's so stupid that she took the Pepsi challenge and chose Dr. Pepper.

Yo mama's so stupid that she thought Grape Nuts was an STD.

Yo mama's so stupid that she asked me what yield meant, I said "Slow down" and she said "What... does.... yield... mean?"

Yo mama's so stupid that she put a phone up her butt and thought she was making a booty call.

Yo mama's so stupid that she put on her glasses to watch 20/20.

Yo mama's so stupid that she climbed over a glass wall to see what was behind it.

Yo mama's so stupid that she failed a survey.

Yo mama's so stupid, she went to the aquarium to buy a Blu-Ray.

Yo mama's so stupid that she thought brownie points were coupons for a bake sale.

Yo mama's so stupid that when the computer said "Press any key to continue", she couldn't find the 'Any' key.

Yo mama's so stupid that she thought Tupac Shakur was a Yiddish holiday.

Yo mama's so stupid that when I was drowning and yelled for a life saver, she said "Cherry or Grape?"

Yo mama's so stupid that I saw her jumping up and down, asked what she was doing, and she said she drank a bottle of medicine and forgot to shake it.

Yo mama's so stupid that when she locked her keys in the car, it took her all day to get her family out.

Yo mama's so stupid that when she pulled into the drive-thru at McDonald's, she drove through the window.

Yo mama's so stupid that she put 2 quarters in her ears and thought she was listening to 50 cent.

Yo mama's so stupid that in the 'No Child Left Behind' act there's a provision that exempts yo mama.

Yo mama's so stupid that she peels M&M's to make chocolate chip cookies.

Yo mama's so stupid that she leaves the house for the Home Shopping Network.

Yo mama's so stupid that she brought a cup to the movie "Juice."

Yo mama's so stupid that she threw a rock at the ground and missed.

Yo mama's so stupid that she tries to email people by putting envelopes into her computer's DVD drive.

Yo mama's so stupid that when she took an IQ test, the results came out negative.

Yo mama's so stupid that she though Jar-Jar came with Pickles-Pickles.

Yo mama's so stupid that she thought St. Ides was a Catholic church.

Yo mama's so stupid that she thought she needed a token to get on Soul Train.

Yo mama's so stupid, that she thought Moby Dick was an STD.

Yo mama's so stupid that she makes Beavis and Butt-Head look like Nobel Prize winners.

Yo mama's so stupid that she got stabbed at a shootout.

Yo mama's so stupid that she took a umbrella to see Purple Rain.

Yo mama's so stupid that she ordered her sushi well done.

Yo mama's so stupid that she put on a coat to chew Winterfresh gum.

Yo mama's so stupid that she put a quarter in a parking meter and waited for a gumball to come out.

Yo mama's so stupid that she ordered a cheese burger from McDonald's and said "Hold the cheese."

Yo mama's so stupid that she thinks Christmas Wrap is an Eminem holiday album.

Yo mama's so stupid that she ran outside with a purse because she heard there was change in the weather.

Yo mama's so stupid that she wiped her butt before she pooped.

Yo mama's so stupid that she tries to insult you with "yo mama" jokes.

Yo mama's so stupid that she put a peephole in a glass door.

Yo mama's so stupid that I saw her in the frozen food section with a fishing rod.

Yo mama's so stupid that when she heard 90% of all crimes occur around the home, she moved.

Yo mama's so stupid that when she saw a "Wrong Way" sign in her rearview mirror, she turned around.

Yo mama's so stupid that she called the 7-11 to see when they closed.

Yo mama's so stupid that she sold the house to pay the mortgage.

Yo mama's so stupid that when I asked her about X-Men she said "Sure, there's Bobby my first baby daddy, Roger the guy I see on Thursdays..."

Yo mama's so stupid that she took lessons for a player piano.

Yo mama's so stupid that she said "what's that letter after x" and I said Y she said "Cause I wanna know".

Yo mama's so stupid that when she asked me what kinda jeans I wore, I said Guess and she said "Ummm... Levis?"

Yo mama's so stupid that if she spoke her mind, she'd be speechless.

Yo mama's so stupid that she can't make Jello because she can't fit 2 quarts of water in the box.

Yo mama's so stupid that the first time she used a vibrator, she cracked her two front teeth.

Yo mama's so stupid that I saw her walking down the street yelling into an envelope, asked what she was doing, and she said sending a voice mail.

Yo mama's so stupid that she tried to drown a fish.

Yo mama's so stupid that if you gave her a penny for her thoughts, you'd get change.

Yo mama's so stupid that she thought Mick Jagger was a breakfast sandwich!

Yo mama's so stupid that when she heard her neighbor was spanking the monkey, she called the humane society.

Yo mama's so stupid that when she took you to the airport and a sign said "Airport Left," she turned around and went home.

Yo mama's so stupid that she bought a solar-powered flashlight!

Yo mama's so stupid that she thought menopause was a button on the VCR.

Yo mama's so stupid that she picked up the phone and asked "What button do I push?"

Yo mama's so stupid that when she worked at McDonald's and someone ordered small fries, she said "Hey Boss, all the small ones are gone."

Yo mama's so stupid that when her husband lost his marbles she ran to the store and bought him new ones.

Yo mama's so stupid that when they said they were playing craps she went and got toilet paper.

Yo mama's so stupid that when I asked her if she wanted to play one on one, she said "Ok, but what's the teams?"

Yo mama's so stupid that she thinks Johnny Cash is a pay toilet!

Yo mama's so stupid that she thinks socialism means partying!

Yo mama's so stupid that when asked on an application, "Sex?", she marked, "M, F, and wrote sometimes Wednesday too."

Yo mama's so stupid that she thinks deadbeat is a type of music.

Yo mama's so stupid that she put two M&M's in her ears and thought she was listening to Eminem.

Yo mama's so stupid that she wouldn't know up from down if she had three guesses.

Yo mama's so stupid that she once attempted to commit suicide by jumping off a curb.

Yo mama's so stupid that she put on bug spray before going to the flea market.

Yo mama's so stupid that she stole free bread.

Yo mama's so stupid that she locked her keys inside a motorcycle.

Yo mama's so stupid, she drowned in a pensieve.

Yo mama's so stupid, she thinks Sirius Black is a hip hop station on satellite radio.

Yo mama's so stupid she thinks Patronus is a kind of Tequlia.

Yo mama's so dumb she thought that she could talk to snakes if she put parsley on her tongue

Yo mama's so dumb that a Stupify spell actually made her smarter.

Yo mama's so stupid, she thinks the G8 is a Value Meal at McDonald's.

Yo mama's so stupid that she thinks sub-prime is a way to cut steak.

Yo mama's so stupid that when the Borg had to choose between assimilating her and a tree, they chose the tree.

Yo mama's so dumb that she tried to rent a car from The Enterprise.

Yo mama's so dumb that when she found a Vulcan, she tried to call Santa to take him back to the north pole.

Yo mama's so weak-minded that I got her to lead me to Jabba without using a Jedi mind trick!

Yo Mama's so stupid the Borg wouldn't assimilate her!

Yo mama's so dumb that when she was handed the Death Note, she thought they were asking for her autograph.

Yo mama's so stupid that she bought tickets to Xbox Live.

Yo mama's so stupid that whenever someone rings the doorbell, she checks the microwave.

Yo mama's so stupid that when she broke her VCR, she bought a video tape on how to fix your VCR.

Yo mama's so stupid that she tried to drop acid but the car battery fell on her foot.

YO MAMA'S SO UGLY...

I see where you got your looks from...

Yes, I'm sorry about that. If I knew she was yo mama, I'd have thrown her a rope and let her on the Ark. As it was, she scared all of the animals enough that the dinosaurs jumped overboard to escape.

Noah

Yo mama's so ugly, when she tried to enter an ugly contest, they said, "Sorry, no professionals."

Yo mama's so ugly, when she looked out her window, she was arrested for indecent exposure.

Yo mama's so ugly, when she was born, the doctor slapped her mother.

Yo mama's so ugly, when she was born, her mother said, "What a treasure!" and her dad said, "Let's bury it."

Yo mama's so ugly, they didn't give her a costume when she auditioned for Star Wars.

Yo mama's so ugly, she was the stand-in for Jabba the Hutt.

Yo mama's so ugly, people put her photograph in the basement to scare away mice.

Yo mama's so ugly, she could make a blind man cry.

Yo mama's so ugly, boomerangs won't return.

Yo mama's so ugly, she could make a freight train take a dirt road.

Yo mama's so ugly, when she cries, the tears refuse to run down her face.

Yo mama's so ugly, her psychiatrist makes her lie face down.

Yo mama's so ugly, they put her picture on a milk carton and it immediately spoiled.

Yo mama's so ugly, they put her picture on a poster for abstinence.

Yo mama's so ugly, she scared away the monster from Alien.

Yo mama's so ugly, she never has to dress up for Halloween.

Yo mama's so ugly, she went into a haunted house and the ghosts moved out.

Yo mama's so ugly, when she walks into the bank, they turn off the surveillance cameras.

Yo mama's so ugly, she has to tie a pork chop around her neck to get the dogs to play with her.

Yo mama's so ugly, the government moved Halloween to her birthday.

Yo mama's so ugly, when she takes a bath, the water jumps out.

Yo mama's so ugly, when she goes to the beach, she causes a mass panic—among the fish.

Yo mama's so ugly, she turned Medusa to stone.

Yo mama's so ugly, when she went to a haunted house she came back with a paycheck.

Yo mama's so ugly, when I took her to the zoo the guy at the gate said thanks for bringing her back.

Yo mama's so ugly, people at the circus pay to not see her.

Yo mama's so ugly, her pillow cries at night.

Yo mama's so ugly, people hang her picture from the rear view mirror so their radios don't get stolen.

Yo mama's so ugly, people dress up as her on Halloween.

Yo mama's so ugly, when she goes to the beach, cats try to bury her.

Yo mama's so ugly, she scares the cockroaches out of the house.

Yo mama's so ugly, people within 50 yards don't have to worry about mosquito bites.

Yo mama's so ugly, your father takes her to work so he doesn't have to kiss her goodbye.

Yo mama's so ugly, she has to creep up on the bath water.

Yo mama's so ugly, Santa Claus can't get the reindeer to stop at her house.

Yo mama's so ugly, the Tooth Fairy died of fright when your mama started snoring.

Yo mama's so ugly, her shadow ran away.

Yo mama's so ugly she frightened a legion of Klingons away.

Yo mama's so ugly that when she went to a beautician it took 12 hours... to get a quote!

Yo mama's so ugly that she looked out the window and got arrested for mooning.

Yo mama's so ugly that she scared the crap out of the toilet.

Yo mama's so ugly that... well... look at you!

Yo mama's so ugly that when she looks in the mirror, the reflection looks back and shakes its head.

Yo mama's so ugly that she looks like she's been in a dryer filled with rocks.

Yo mama's so ugly that she makes blind children cry.

Yo mama's so ugly that she fell down the ugly ladder and didn't miss a step.

Yo mama's so ugly that the last time I saw something that looked like her, I pinned a tail on it.

Yo mama's so ugly that we put her in the kennel when we go on vacation.

Yo mama's so ugly that her shadow ran away from her.

Yo mama's so ugly that she could scare the flies off a garbage truck.

Yo mama's so ugly that her birth certificate contained an apology letter from the condom factory.

Yo mama's so ugly that her mom had to be drunk to breast feed her.

Yo mama's so ugly that even Rice Krispies won't talk to her!

Yo mama's so ugly that when she drove past area 51, she was thought to be extraterrestrial life. They took her away never to be seen again.

Yo mama's so ugly that they pay her to put her clothes on in strip joints

Yo mama's so ugly, a Klingon warrior hit her in the face with a bat'leth, and it shattered.

Yo mama's so ugly that she made an onion cry!

Yo mama's so ugly that when I last saw a mouth like hers, it had a hook in it.

Yo mama's so ugly that she gets 364 extra days to dress up for Halloween!

Yo mama's so ugly that when she plays Mortal Kombat, Scorpion tells her to "Stay Over There!"

Yo mama's so ugly that neither Jacob nor Edward wants her on their team.

Yo mama's so ugly that they push her face into dough to make gorilla cookies.

Yo mama's so ugly that she gives Freddy Kreuger nightmares.

Yo mama's so ugly that when she walks in the kitchen, the rats jump on the table and start screaming.

Yo mama's so ugly that even Bill Clinton wouldn't sleep with her.

Yo mama's so ugly that when she was born, the doctor slapped her AND her parents!

Yo mama's so ugly that she didn't get hit with the ugly stick, she got hit by the whole damn tree.

Yo mama's so ugly that she has 7 years bad luck just trying to look at herself in the mirror.

Yo mama's so ugly that she practices birth control by leaving the lights on.

Yo mama's so ugly that she'd scare the monster out of Loch Ness.

Yo mama's so ugly that it looks like she's been bobbing for French fries.

Yo mama's so ugly that when she looks in the mirror it says "viewer discretion is advised."

Yo mama's so ugly that she can look up a camel's butt and scare the hump off of it.

Yo mama's so ugly that when she moved into the projects, all her neighbors chipped in for curtains.

Yo mama's so ugly that Santa pays an elf to drop off her gifts at Christmas.

Yo mama's so ugly that if she was a scarecrow, the corn would run away.

Yo mama's so ugly that she could be the poster child for birth control.

Yo mama's so ugly that when she went to Taco Bell everyone ran for the border.

Yo mama's so ugly that her face is blurred on her driver's license.

Yo mama's so ugly that when she walked out of her house, the neighbors called animal control.

Yo mama's so ugly that the FCC requires her face to be blurred when she's on TV, because of decency rules.

Yo mama's so ugly that a sculpture of her face is used when torturing prisoners at Guantanamo Bay.

Yo mama's so ugly that government intelligence agencies have to pixelize her face when spying on her.

Yo mama's so ugly that she's never seen herself 'cause the mirrors keep breaking.

Yo mama's so ugly that when she was born she was put in an incubator with tinted windows.

Yo mama's so ugly that she put the Boogie Man out of business!

Yo mama's so ugly that she made Barack Obama lose hope!

Yo mama was such an ugly baby that her parents had to feed her with a slingshot.

Yo mama's so ugly, even a Dementor wouldn't kiss her!

Yo mama's so ugly that the Whomping Willow saw her and died.

Yo Mama's so ugly, everybody calls her "She-Who-Must-Not-Be-Naked"

Yo mama's so ugly that the Dementor's Kiss was swapped out for a hearty handshake and a promise to give her a call sometime.

Yo Mama's so ugly that even Voldemort won't say her name.

Yo mama's so ugly that she lost a beauty contest to a Mountain Troll.

Yo mama's so ugly the Fremen on Arrakis use her to keep the Dune Worms at bay.

Yo mama's so ugly that when she walked into Gringotts Wizarding Bank, they gave her a job application.

Yo mama's so ugly she turned the Basilisk to stone.

Yo mama's so ugly that Voldemort took one look at her and killed HIMSELF!

Yo mama's so ugly, she thought that Hogwarts were the growths on her thigh.

Yo mama's so ugly that as a baby they had to use the Confundus Charm so the family would play with her.

Yo mama's so ugly that when she asked Crabbe to take her to the Yule Ball, he decided to go with Goyle instead!

Yo mama's so ugly that you could put lipstick on a pig and it would look ten times better than her!

Yo mama's so ugly that Wuher the Mos Eisley bartender from Star Wars said 'We don't serve your kind here'.

Yo mama's so ugly that the term 'bantha poodoo' wasn't used metaphorically with reference to her.

Yo mama's so ugly that Dr. Evazan looks like a male supermodel next to her.

Yo mama's so ugly that she made Doctor McCoy say "Damnit Jim, I'm a doctor, not a Zoologist!"

Yo mama's so ugly that she's probably a Shi'ido Clawdite that stays in her regular form all the time.

Yo Mama's so ugly even Data would need special eye goggles to look at her.

Yo mama's so ugly her Kazon hairdo is an improvement!

Yo Mama's so ugly even a Ferengi would dress her in clothes.

Yo Mama's so ugly she did the truly impossible: she made Captain James T Kirk go limp.

Yo mama's so ugly, that Pythagoras wouldn't touch her with a 3-4-5 triangle.

Yo mama's so ugly that she made Spike Spiegel choke on his cigarette.

Yo mama's so ugly, she can't even have tentacle porn sex.

Yo mama's so ugly that she's like a Death Note. Get someone to look at her, and they'll die!

Yo mama's so ugly, Saya thought she was a Chiropteran.

Yo mama's so ugly that when Kakashi looked directly at her, he lost an eye.

Yo mama's so ugly that she makes Orochimaru look beautiful.

Yo mama's so ugly, people think the circus is in town.

Yo mama's so ugly, she works as a hit man for the mafia.

Yo mama's so ugly, the government uses her as a nuclear deterrent.

Yo mama's so ugly, they used her image as the final boss in Donkey Kong. Nobody's beat it yet.

Yo mama's so ugly, it's her face on that video tape in The Ring.

Yo mama's so ugly, Saruman based the Uruk Hai on her face.

Yo mama's so ugly, Sauron jumped in the fires of Mount Doom to escape her ever-watchful eye.

Yo mama's so ugly, she has a blast radius rating.

Yo mama's so ugly, even orcs shake their heads in pity.

ABOUT THE AUTHOR

BIO:

Guy Anthony De Marco is a nocturnal Bram Stoker Award® nominated author living in the shadow of the Rocky Mountains. He writes across multiple genres and in multiple mediums. An award-winning author, he is a member of SFWA, IAMTW, HWA, ASCAP, the Science Fiction Poetry Association, Rocky Mountain Fiction Writers, and Northern Colorado Writers. Additional information can be found at en.wikipedia.org/wiki/Guy_Anthony_De_Marco and at his author site, http://www.GuyAnthonyDeMarco.com, or participating on panels at numerous conventions throughout the year.

LINKS:

http://guyanthonydemarco.com/

http://en.wikipedia.org/wiki/Guy_Anthony_De_Marco

http://www.isfdb.org/cgi-bin/ea.cgi?136687

SOCIAL MEDIA:

https://www.facebook.com/SpeculativeFictionAuthor

https://twitter.com/GuyADeMarco

http://www.goodreads.com/author/show/5768074.Guy_Anthony_De_Marco

SELECTED WORKS:

Novels & Collections

Life & Everything Too (Warped Mind Press, 2012)

Ancient Terrors, Volumes 1-8 (Villainous Press, 2013)

Odd Places (Yurei Press, 2012, ISBN 9781622250040)

The Bride, (Macabre Press, 2014)

The Dynasty Sentinel (TPC, 2014)

Fury Within (Yurei Press, 2015)

Ultimate "Yo Mama" Joke Book (Villainous Press, 2013)

Ultimate "Blonde" Joke Book (Villainous Press, 2013)

Anthologies

Dead Meat (The Help Anthology, 2008)

Steaks (Every Day Fiction Two, 2008, ISBN 9780981058429)

Steaks (Daily Bites of Flesh 2011, 2010, ISBN 9781617060182)

Monsters (Daily Bites of Flesh 2011, 2010, ISBN 9781617060182)

Absolute Truths and Outright Lies (Collection, 2011, Yurei Press, ISBN 9781622250011)

The Prize (GalaxyFest Omnibus Limited 1st Edition, 2012, ISBN 9781470088958)

For Christmas, I Made My Mother Cry (Angels Cried, Charity Anthology for Sandy Hook, 2012)

Letter from Melinda (Letters to Santa, May-December Publications, 2012)

A Gift of Ben-Wa Balls (Pill Hill Daily Flash 2013)

Annoying the Chief (Pill Hill Daily Flash 2013)

Stuff Migrates (Pill Hill Daily Flash 2013)

Rabbits (50 Shades of Decay, 2013)

Seeds (Dark Bits, Apokrupha, 2013)

Steaks (Barnyard Horror, 2013)

Member of the Herd (Barnyard Horror, 2013)

Lyssa's New Friend (Twist of Fate, Navigator Books, 2013, ASIN B00DQ533QE)

Made in United States
Orlando, FL
14 April 2022

16823676R00082